Also by Jim Edgar

<u>Bad Cat</u>

MY CAT HATES YOU

Jim Edgar

Illustrations by Beth McNelley

A Fireside Book
Published by Simon & Schuster
New York London Toronto Sydney

Dedicated to

the

MyCatHatesYou.com

community

Be afraid. Be very afraid!

Tornado! Earthquake! Tsunami! These words strike fear into our hearts, for they kill without warning, reason, or malice.

Yet, as evidenced in the following pages, there is something more terrifying than a random act of God. And you probably have one in your house as you read this, scoping you out like a sniper in Bosnia.

I proudly present to you this collection of evidence of your very own <u>Felis catus</u> engaged in what they do best: **hating you!**

Thanks to the help of countless victims worldwide, I am able to bring to light a conspiracy against mankind that reaches around the globe and, as some posit, perhaps into other dimensions!

Though the names have been changed to protect the guilty, the following images are terrifyingly real. Keep this book out of reach of childen and especially cats. They don't need encouragement.

That is all.

—Jim

Hudson

"Hey! I found Nemo!"

1

Vah Vah

"Up up . . . and away!"

2

Piggy

"This guy has *no* sense of humor."

Ginger

"There's a pod back here
with your name on it."

Boop & Kiki

"I know the Visa bill is here somewhere.
Strip clubs, here we come!"

Steve & Frog

"Frog is my copilot!"

INFAMOUS FELINE MUG SHOTS

Los Angeles Kitten Court
Feline 8980-KIRO

Alias: Li'l Badass
Charge: Late-night dissonant meowing
       without a license

Spot

"Whew! They didn't shrink after all!"

Suzuki

"Damn! I thought it said Booze!"

Castro

"Just because I live with you does not mean I like fruit!"

Nickname: Timothy Leery

Voted most likely to: get all your sisters
                    pregnant—twice

Minge

"Nobody up here but us killers."

Damiana

"Welcome to the Dark Side!"

Baxter

"Steve Irwin lied to me . . . teeth hurt!"

INFAMOUS FELINE MUG SHOTS

Reno Vagrancy Enforcement
Smith-Kerns 002-33

Name: Little F'n Demon
Charge: Criminal catnapping on
       the designer comforter

Pearl

"A Jew, a Muslim, and a Buddhist walk into a bar . . ."

Murphy

"Do I kill it . . . or screw it?"

Zisou

"Sweet and sour rice coming right up!"

Kali

"I can't stalk anything in this!"

DISOBEDIENCE SCHOOL YEARBOOK

Nickname: the Fearsome Foursome

Voted most likely to: hold the fridge hostage and demand tuna ransom

Chauncey

"I think this guy's batteries are dead!"

Obi-Wan

"Why do I get a bad feeling about this?"

Clinger

"When you are done swabbing the deck, I am going to hoist your mainsail!"

23

The Triad

"I say we get rid of the orange one and eat all his food!"

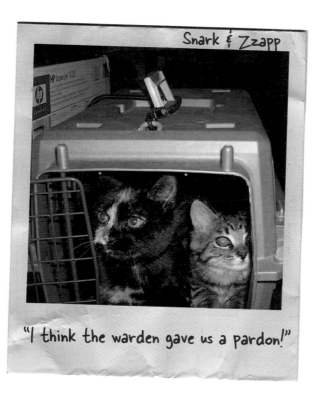

Snark & Zzapp

"I think the warden gave us a pardon!"

Spitzer

"I have no excuses, only apologies . . ."

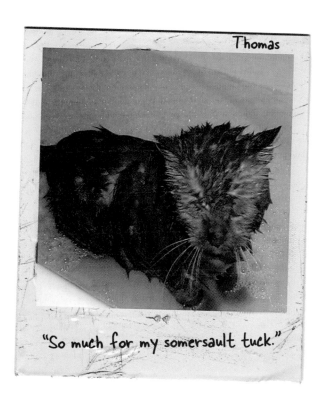

Thomas

"So much for my somersault tuck."

INFAMOUS FELINE MUG SHOTS

ASPCA Chapter 14
Case 09-A0034

Name: Vincent "Claws" Vintucci
Charge: Hogging the front table
at Bada Bing

Connie

"What happens in the box . . .
stays in the box!"

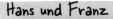
Hans und Franz

"To properly do Kitty Reiki, you must apply claws to back as such!"

Sarah

"I think that last toke
    killed two of my lives."

Skittles & Marx

"I love this Brazilian waxing thing!"

Capt. Stubing

"Didn't I kill you last week?"

Nickname: the Teflon Tom

Voted most likely to: await trial in the
                      pound for breaking
                      and entering

34

Angela

"Some Tabasco and my
lunch will be complete!"

Katanga & Lord

"Let's forget that ever happened,
eh, Katanga?"

Lily

"One more bowl of the dry stuff
and I am lighting this sucker!"

Arnold Layne

"I did something else
   under the mistletoe!"

Ash & Smokey

"We feel your butt has gotten too big for this chair."

Cramden

"Trust me, it's not a paper jam."

41

Clause

"The one that got away was this big!"

42

Darth

"But mine was THIS big!"

Ganesh

"Hey! I can almost touch my eyebrows!"

Ruben & Simon

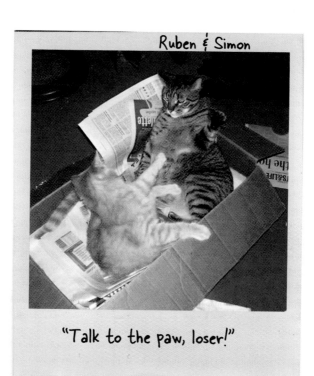

"Talk to the paw, loser!"

Hellion

"The mailman is here! Hand sandwich!"

Josie

"Crap! This one has a LoJack too!"

Harvey

"What would Pooh Bear do?"

INFAMOUS FELINE MUG SHOTS

SEARS Anti-Fraud Squad
Bad Repairman BR-2998-3.g

Alias: "Maytag Manny"
Charge: Bogus appliance repair
without a bogus license

Lamont

"Finally my plan is complete!"

Madison

"He speaks no evil. Me? I DO evil!"

Willis & Reba

"Wake up, you! Where's the Jager?!"

52

Big Mac

"I forgot the parental control code again."

Darnell

"Get out of here, kid . . . ya bother me."

Linda

"Don't you think this empty nest
thing is getting kinda old?"

Grace

"Good morning. Where's my milk!?"

Wheezie

"I only eat the ones I love."

57

INFAMOUS FELINE MUG SHOTS

Dade County Animal Control
015504

Alias: Wizard of Wyeth Street
Charge: Selling illusory cat treats

Insulin

"You want a piece of this, punk?"

Maxime

"When I go to heaven . . .
at least I will never see you there."

Marnie

"These always taste better on catnip!"

Meiko

"Go ahead—ring my bell."

Nala

"You killed my father! Prepare to die!"

Abbott & Costello

"Come on, Abbott, gimme a smoke!"

Pibb—Mr. Pibb

"On the first day of Christmas . . .
I gave my owner fleas!"

Rasputin

"When the clock strikes midnight . . .
you bring me their heads on a plate!"

Sam

"No accidents for 190 days,
  but no silver either."

Crandal

"Who needs hair when
you have sex appeal!?"

Tycho & "friend"

"In the dark we can't tell
the difference."

INFAMOUS FELINE MUG SHOTS

Tijuana Terrorist Alert Team
Docket 388-Juárez

Name: José Juárez, aka El Gato Puto
Charge: Borracho y loco, ese!

Vito

"Two feet . . . to . . . freedom!"

Ba'al

"One ounce of pure evil coming right up!"

Chadwick the Great!

"In my dreams I'm a mountain lion!"

Glenda

"You get extra beads at Mardi Gras for showing eight nipples."

Scully

"Welcome to my hallway of hell!"

Sludge

"Strangely, this feels distinctively
different from your buttocks!"

Nickname: Arecibo Ann

Voted most likely to: make contact with evil
extraterrestrials

HOlmes

"This medicine tastes like crap!"

Boo

"Get that tongue over here
and give me a bath!"

Tino

"When I count to three, you will go
buy me a new scratching post . . ."

Tux the Clown

"If you don't mind the splinters,
I'll do anything for five bucks."

INFAMOUS FELINE MUG SHOTS

Seattle Port Police
Detainee 400-261

Name: Mr. Sunshine
Charge: Paying dockworkers to steal
the latest tanning beds from Britain

The Freak

"I am NOT paranoid,
  they really are watching me."

Steve Austin

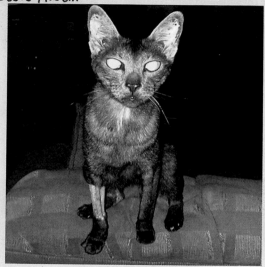

"They made me better than
before—faster . . . stronger . . ."

Evil Juniper

"Come on, human. You're pooping
outside from now on."

The Massive

"Where is Dr. Atkins when I need him?"

José

"Mmmm . . .mezcal!
One worm in—100 out!"

Critter

"Awww . . . I always thought I
came from my mommy's tummy!"

Drambuie

"You know, if you lost weight I
would not have to help you bathe."

Chone

"Beer! Beer! Beer!
Beer! Beer! Beer!"

Sophie & Creampuff

"Crap . . . I forgot the safe word!"

Falk

"Does this make my ass look big?"

Lucas

"Yoda! Help me! Yoda! Help me!"

Montgomery

"Exxxcelllent!"

Aleister

"When the Troll of Althron slays the Dragon of Hasselhoff, all will fear the Rise of ALEISTER!"

Zminou

"I saved a hairball for ya, friend—o!"

Eli

"It's good! The Giants win!"

Prowler

"The ball says things don't
look so good for you."

Blue

"O say can you seeee?"

Jacamo

"I'm wearing a damned tie . . .
    Can I come in for dinner now?"

"I was supposed to turn into a sabertoofs!"

Manson

For Sale: One Evil Cat—New in Box

Princeton

"Our audit shows that you are too stupid to defraud us. Good day, sir!"

Bandit

"The spellbook said vampire BAT.
What gives?"

Nickname: the Proctologist

Voted most likely to: examine you while
                      you are passed out

Midget

"The irony is—I'm a dude."

Piglet

"Put the champagne in the ice bucket and get the hell out!"

The Tank

"How come there are only the
two of us at this party?"

"It's a raid! Flush the 'nip!"

INFAMOUS FELINE MUG SHOTS

Ontario Feline Sweep Program
Catch 809: 015

Name: Crinkle, aka Big Bob
Charge: Passing self off as porn star
without adequate evidence

Cabrone

"Martha Stewart you are not!"

Muttley

"Word of advice: do not piss off
voodoo priestess in New Orleans."

Little Slim

"I sure hope I got her number!"

Benedict

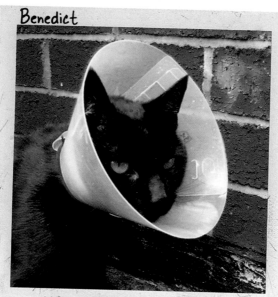

"Forty bucks and all I
get is Radio Belgrade?!"

Nickname: Brokeback Bennie

Voted most likely to: come out of the closet
                      before graduation.

Boris

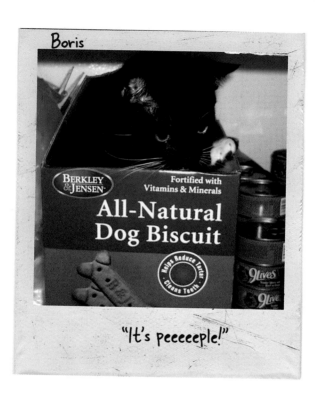

"It's peeeeeple!"

Wee-Bey

"I am the Cat in the Hat . . . Box."

Jabba

"Funny, I've never been invited
to Thanksgiving dinner before!"

Johnny

"Heeerrre's Johnny!!!"

Baron & Miki

"This is legal in California!"

Ivan & Boris

"I see you are in the fraternity too!"

Stephen

"Damn you, Victoria's Secret,
and your never-ending G-string!"

INFAMOUS FELINE MUG SHOTS

Renaissance Faire
Stockade Holes 3 & 5

Alias: King Wodewick & Squire
Charge: Stormed the castle and
pooped in the moat

Mick & Mack

"Put it on Air Fluff and get in!"

Sayid

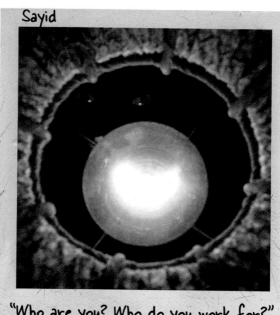

"Who are you? Who do you work for?"

Sparks

"Looks like I got the good half!"

INFAMOUS FELINE MUG SHOTS

Drug Enforcement Agency
Subject: TOPANGA—256

Alias: Mister Big Green Buds
Charge: Pushing low-grade oregano
        as "Killer Kind Buds" catnip

Guinness & Smokey

"How was I to know his mother
really WAS a half-breed!?"

Gunther

"Go, my legions! Bring me Friskies!"

Chelsea

"Do I look like I care?"

Simba

"What do you mean there
are no feline Olympics?"

Jaffa

"Go away! This is MY jungle fortress!"

Gojira

"Officer Gojira to base.
            Stakeout in effect."

Jed

"I've got two words for you:
Body Acceptance."

135

INFAMOUS FELINE MUG SHOTS

Malibu Neighborhood Watch
Case P0092J

Alias: Anti-Welcome to the Neighborhood Gang
Charge: Boring new tenants to sleep with long
stories, then stealing their food

Moab

"I usually don't show up on film."

Listerine

"BAG-1   ME-O"

Malley

"The next item for bidding, folks:
one Patsy Cline walking boot!"

Darcy & Lucy

"Stop praying to the tulip and give me a back rub!"

Mister Lee

"This is what I get for being too high."

The Baron

"New neighbors . . . NEW MEAT!"

Vader

"The Dark Side has always appealed to me."

143

Pancho

"Now who's the big man, huh?"

INFAMOUS FELINE MUG SHOTS

Vatican City Interdiction Dept.
Prisoner 70034

Alias: the Prophet of Palermo
Charge: Promising fast track to cat
       heaven in exchange for cream

Pokey

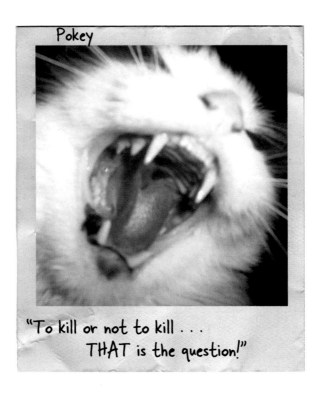

"To kill or not to kill . . .
        THAT is the question!"

Alistair & Puddy

"The name of this story:
'The Telltale Fart.'"

Thompson

"The only thing magic about this carpet is my ability not to puke on it."

148

Ursula

"Hunting at the lodge would be more
fun if I could just shoot YOU!"

WunderKat!

"I plead . . . insanity?!"

150

Black Murphy

"Finally! The chromosome
for opposable thumbs!"

Gnosis Monkey

"I'm ready for my close-up."

Surafel

"Hold still while I finish your noose."

153

Kinky

"This is my punishment for voting for Ralph Nader!"

154

Kismet

"They accept my lifestyle—
                        why can't you?"

Lupe

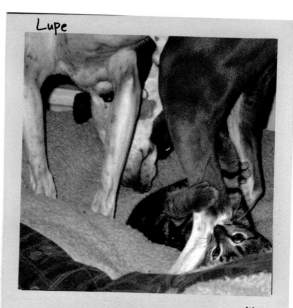

"Yes, it DOES taste like chicken!"

INFAMOUS FELINE MUG SHOTS

North Pole White-Collar Crime Div.
Reg I.D. Rummy-09

Alias: Old Rummy
Charge: Impersonated Santa at Macy's
        and beat up elves

Buttersworth

"You call that a conjugal visit?"

Boots

"I hope you won't mind if I season these."

150

Beelzebub

"Four weeks of pottery class and you insult me with this?"

Korglar

"We all look like this in my galaxy."

Grimley

"You can't keep me down forever!"

INFAMOUS FELINE MUG SHOTS

Waco Wacko Ward
354-2294/09

Alias: the Maude Squad
Charge: Assaulting little old lady cats
        and blaming voices in their heads

Zooger

"Finally I am the one in control."

Queeg

"Give me a kiss and let's get
this suicide pact under way!"

Dan Rather

"Bleeechhh!"

Nickname: El Maestro

Voted most likely to: become top dog jockey
of the neighborhood

Frisco

"I'm ready! Are we there yet?
I said, I'm ready! Hurry up—let's go!"

Plato & Socrates

"Don't mess with us,
we're zombies!"

Locutus

"I think I am in the wrong book."

Spud & Crabtree

"Trust us, we need every inch."

Gibson & Kelly

"What we have here is
a failure to communicate!"

Thumb

"Give me five minutes with it
and I'll make it talk!"

Machine Gun Kelly

"You still alive, eh? I can fix that!"

Nickname: the Cleaner

Voted most likely to: sell all your stuff
on eBay

Slick

"I said PRAWNS, not pawns."

Wellington

"Competitive Eating Contests?
No problem . . . I have AUTOFEEDER!"

Ducky

"Your king o' the hill days are over."

Jeshua

"Uhh, he's not here. You can just
leave a message with me."

179

Ahab

"Eight days in the biosphere
and I am still here, folks!"

Polenta

"Are we celebrating my birthday
or an increase in your IQ?"

INFAMOUS FELINE MUG SHOTS

Odessa County Lockup
Zed-90-88

Alias: Felix "Freshmaker" Stone
Charge: Joyriding in the baby stroller
and leaving the baby on the porch

Oswald

"This is how I cut the rug."

Morgan

"I just wish I knew who he was."

184

Zoie

"Now where's that damned mousicle?"

Zaven

"So much for that cat's cradle thing."

Franklin

"Lance Armstrong does it with
one testicle. I do it with none."

Mia

"This is what I think of your car insurance."

Haise

"Houston, we have a problem!
   This is not my new litter box."

Nickname: Brother Bast

Voted most likely to: start an old-time
                      kitty revival church

Franq

"When I say 'ho, ho, ho,' why do you always turn around, lady?"

Birba

"I hate to leave you out here,
    but there can be only one."

Oliver

"All this over-the-hill
stuff and no Viagra?"

Nader

"Recycle THIS!"

Dallas

"Damn you, Mister Big Green Buds!
This is nothing but oregano, man!"

Celeste & Pokey

"We'd like to see YOU eat this stuff."

Coco

"Please, open me before Christmas."

Tick   Tick   Tick   Tick   Tick

197

Chevy

"If this doesn't get me a lady,
I'm going to match.com!"

Rusty & crew

"Two against one, huh?
All right, let's get it on!"

Dr. Travis

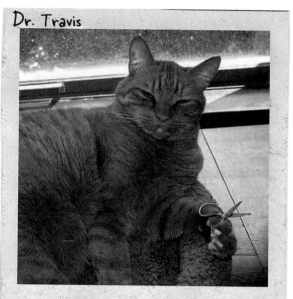

"Turnabout is fair play. Let's see 'em!"

Tara

"Safari was very, very good to me."

Buddha Fu

"Gravity has no power over Buddha Fu!"

Buzz

"Everyone needs a little
Happy Feet now and then!"

Walter

"Yeah, yeah, swear to tell the truth.
The devil made me do it, OKAY?!"

INFAMOUS FELINE MUG SHOTS

Feral Abatement, Prescott, AZ
Lockup C-Block 54/4

Alias: Prescott Pied Piper
Charge: Ran rodent rodeo

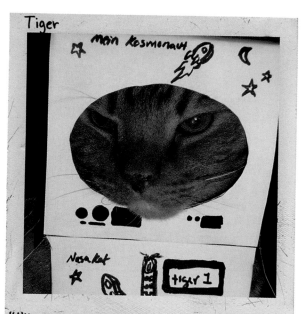

Tiger

mein kosmonaut

Nasa kat

tiger 1

"I'll do anything to escape your gravity!"

Lasky

"I wear the pants around here."

Tenzin

"Belly pounce in 3 . . . 2 . . . 1!"

Rufus

"Ah, the good life . . .
    too bad it's only a set."

Bean

"It may be the booze talking, but
I am pretty sure I can kick your ass."

Anna Nicole

"There's only one way down: my way!"

Pooper

"D'ya mind? I'm kinda
reading this right now."

Crusty

"I didn't get the name Cauliflower
Cat by mowing lawns, chum!"

213

Nikki

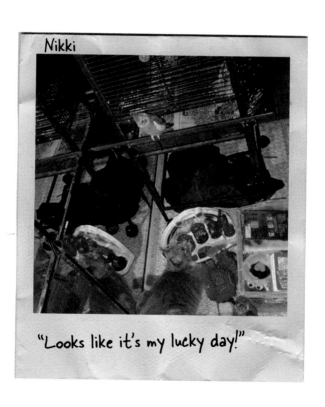

"Looks like it's my lucky day!"

Lebedeff

"Give me borscht or give me death!"

Pringles

"So I'm home late—what of it?!"

INFAMOUS FELINE MUG SHOTS

Area 51 Containment Unit
Holding Tank GG-032

Alias: Mysterio X
Charge: Interdimensional traveling
and scaring the baby

Toulousse

"Must . . . get . . . clam chowder!"

"Your miniature gay club
impresses me not!"

Kanat

"Flowers again? You must really be
in the doghouse, buddy!"

Paige

"Polygamy looks better on TV."

Scrumpy

"I know what you did last night."

Bethany

"I ate them! I ate them all!
Muahahaha!"

Bangladesh

"Why bother naming me when
I never listen to you anyway?"

Taster

"Why does it have your
picture under 'Loser'?"

Clan McClan

"The DNA tests will clear me.
Next week on <u>Maury!</u>"

"One! One ugly-ass cat! Ah-ah-ah-ah!"

Rusty

"I was going to get a tattoo of your name, but I forgot your name."

Nickname: Niblet
Voted most likely to: wreak havoc in
                     Christmastown

The Rixter

"Identity theft starts here."

Mister Sniffles

"Why didn't they build this thing with belly support?"

Gletta & Kenniecat

"We are the yin and the yang."

Hansel

"I'm not opening this
until I see a warrant!"

Reed

"Your homage is accepted."

234

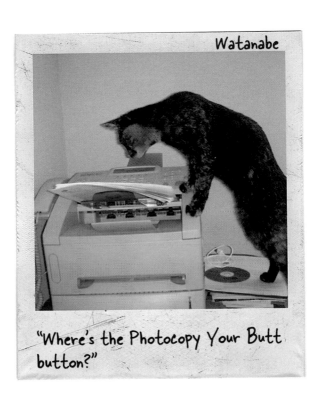

Watanabe

"Where's the Photocopy Your Butt button?"

Cleo

"Mirror, mirror on the counter, when do I get my 10-lb. flounder?"

Ashley

"You need some friends—I am getting tired of beating you."

Decker

"Management says they like my style."

Priss

"You have to come out sometime!"

Fribbit

"No more baby. Only Fribbit!"

Farnum

"Screw trick or treat.
we came for the cash!"

Major Gitmo

"Bubba and Princess did the job.
I just drove the getaway car."

Karl & Maik

"We heard about the new kitten,
and we are not happy about it."

243

Samantha

"Are you trying to tell me I'm fat?"

Nickname: Grumpus
Voted most likely to: be so grumpy he
                      makes toys grumpy

Rip van Winkle

"Go away. I'm undercover!"